W9-AVM-377

PowerKiDS
Readers

Happy Holidays!
¡Felices Fiestas!

Hanukkah
Janucá

Josie Keogh

PowerKiDS
press.

New York

Published in 2013 by The Rosen Publishing Group, Inc.
29 East 21st Street, New York, NY 10010

First Edition

Editor: Amelie von Zumbusch
Book Design: Andrew Povolny

Traducción al español: Eduardo Alamán

Photo Credits: Cover Tome Le Goff/Photodisc/Getty Images; p. 5 Pam Ostrow/Photolibrary/Getty Images; p. 7 iStockphoto/Thinkstock; p. 9 Michael Cogliantry/Photodisc/Getty Images; p. 11 Hemera/Thinkstock; p. 13 © iStockphoto.com/Sarah Bossert; p. 15 © iStockphoto.com/Sean Locke; p. 17 Jupiterimages/Photos.com/Thinkstock; p. 19 Fuse/Getty Images; p. 21 Jupiterimages/Photos.com/Thinkstock; p. 23 Katrina Wittkamp/Photodisc/Getty Images.

Library of Congress Cataloging-in-Publication Data

Keogh, Josie.
 Hanukkah = Janucá / by Josie Keogh ; translated by Eduardo Alamán. — 1st ed.
    p. cm. — (Powerkids readers: happy holidays! / ¡Felices Fiestas!)
 Includes index.
 ISBN 978-1-4488-9969-2 (library binding)
 1. Hanukkah—Juvenile literature. I. Alamán, Eduardo. II. Title.
 BM695.H3K4613 2013
 296.4'35—dc23
                                        2012022317

Websites: Due to the changing nature of Internet links, PowerKids Press has developed an online list of websites related to the subject of this book. This site is updated regularly. Please use this link to access the list: www.powerkidslinks.com/pkrhh/hanuk/

Manufactured in the United States of America

CPSIA Compliance Information: Batch #W13PK3: For Further Information contact Rosen Publishing, New York, New York at 1-800-237-9932

Contents

Contenido

Hanukkah lasts eight days.

Janucá dura ocho días.

4

5

It honors what took place in the Jewish Temple.

Janucá honra lo sucedido en el Templo de Jerusalén.

7

The oil lasted for eight nights!

¡El aceite de la lámpara duró ocho días y ocho noches!

That is why you eat foods
fried in oil.

_____

Es por eso que, en Janucá,
comes comida frita en aceite.

Latkes are made of potatoes.

Los **latkes** están hechos de patatas.

13

Light the **menorah**!

¡Enciende el **janukiá**
o candelabro!

The **shamash** is in the middle of it.

El **shamas** es la vela que está en el centro.

There are gifts.

En Janucá se dan regalos.

19

Spin the dreidel!

¡Juega con el *dreidel*!

You can win gelt.

Puedes ganar "guelt", o dinero de Janucá.

WORDS TO KNOW / PALABRAS QUE DEBES SABER

latke	menorah	shamash
(el) latke	(el) janukiá	(el) shamash

INDEX

ÍNDICE